HOPE

6 Studies for Individuals or Groups

Receiving Hope *from God*

[Dale & Juanita Ryan]

Letting God Be God Bible Studies

InterVarsity Press
Downers Grove, Illinois

InterVarsity Press
P.O. Box 1400, Downers Grove, IL 60515-1426
World Wide Web: www.ivpress.com
E-mail: mail@ivpress.com

InterVarsity Press® is the book-publishing division of InterVarsity Christian Fellowship/USA®, a student movement active on campus at hundreds of universities, colleges and schools of nursing in the United States of America, and a member movement of the International Fellowship of Evangelical Students. For information about local and regional activities, write Public Relations Dept., InterVarsity Christian Fellowship/USA, 6400 Schroeder Rd., P.O. Box 7895, Madison, WI 53707-7895.

Cover photograph: Michael Goss

Cover logo and interior icons: Roberta Polfus

ISBN 0-8308-2071-X

Printed in the United States of America ∞

19 18 17 16 15 14 13 12 11 10 9 8 7 6 5 4 3 2 1
16 15 14 13 12 11 10 09 08 07 06 05 04 03 02 01

CONTENTS

Introduction: Receiving Hope from God

Why are you downcast, O my soul?
Why so disturbed within me?
Put your hope in God,
for I will yet praise him,
my Savior and my God.
(Psalm 42:11)

Without hope, life is difficult to sustain. Hope keeps us going. It keeps us from giving up when outward appearances might lead us to despair. Hope is the capacity to trust that there is a bigger picture which we cannot always see—a bigger picture that gives meaning to life's events whether they are big or little, glorious or difficult. Clearly, we need hope. We need it every day. We cannot go on without it.

We know that hope that has weak foundations is nothing more than wishful thinking. And wishful thinking tends to disappear when challenged by life's difficulties. The hope we need is not mere optimism or cheerfulness or looking on the bright side. Those may be good things in their place, but they will not sustain us in the most difficult times of life. We need a hope that is based in deep certainty.

Scripture teaches us that the foundation for hope is God—that God is the God of Hope. When we receive hope from God—when we let God be God in this way—we are basing our hope in the certainty of God's unfailing love. Hope that is deeply rooted in God's loving, active presence with us, is a powerful force in our lives and in this world. This kind of hope is what makes it possible for us to not run away when things are difficult, but rather to stay present to ourselves and others, trusting we will be given the courage and strength we need for the difficulties we face.

Yet there are times in life when all reason for hope seems to vanish—times when our trust in God is shaken. In times like this we may lose our capacity for hope. This can happen to people with great faith as well as to people with only a mustard seed of faith. Fortunately, God understands these times of hopelessness. Scripture is full of stories about people of faith who have lost all hope. Scripture shows us that God responds with gifts of love to people who lose hope. And Scripture reminds us that in those times when all reasons for hope seem to have failed, God is still at work. God's powerful love is unfailing.

The studies in this guide are designed to help you open your hearts and lives to the God of hope. It is our prayer that in the process of working through these studies, God's Spirit will free you to receive God's gift of hope in new ways.

Learning to Let God Be God

The Bible studies in this series are based on three basic convictions. The first of these convictions is that we are by our very nature dependent on our Maker. We need God. We need God's help with the daily challenges of life. We need God's love, peace, forgiveness, guidance and hope. The invitation to "let God be God" is an invitation to let God be who God really is. But it is also an invitation to us to be who we really are—God's deeply loved children.

Second, these studies are based on the conviction that God is willing, ready and eager to be God in our lives. God is not distant, inaccessible or indifferent. Rather, God is actively involved, offering us all that we need. God offers us all the love, strength, hope and peace we need.

Finally, these studies are based on the conviction that the spiritual life begins with receiving from God. What we do when we "let God be God" is receive from God the good gifts that God is eager to give to us. God has offered to love us. We are "letting God be God" when we receive this love. God has offered to guide us. We are "letting God be God" when we receive this guidance. Receiving from God is the starting point of the spiritual life. There is, of course, a place in the Christian journey for giving to God—a place for commitment and dedication. But if we have not learned well to receive from God, then we will almost certainly experience the Christian journey to be full of heavy burdens.

These are basic Christian convictions that closely resemble the first three steps of the twelve steps of Alcoholics Anonymous. The short summary is "I can't. God can. I'll let him." These are spiritual truths that apply to all of our lives. They may seem pretty simple. But most of us find that actually doing them—putting these truths into practice—is anything but simple. The problem is that receiving is not instinctive for most of us. What is instinctive is self-sufficiency, independence and managing by ourselves. What comes naturally is trying harder and trying our hardest. Letting go of this performance-oriented spirituality and allowing ourselves to receive from God will be a challenging adventure for most of us. It is the adventure that is at the heart of these Bible studies.

These Bible studies are designed to help you explore what it means to receive from God—what it means to let God be God in your life. George MacDonald used a wonderful metaphor when talking about the process of learning to receive from God. He said, "There are good things God must delay giving, until his child has a pocket to hold them—until God gets his child to make that pocket" (as cited in Michael R. Phillips, ed., *Discovering the Character of God* [Minneapolis: Bethany House, 1989], p. 156). These studies are designed to help you sew some new pockets that are big enough to hold the abundant good gifts that God has prepared for you.

Getting the Most from These Studies

The guides in this series are designed to assist you to find out what the Bible has to say about God and to grow in your ability to "let God be God" in your life. The passages you study will be thought provoking, challenging, inspiring and very personal. It will become obvious that these studies are not designed merely to convince you of the truthfulness of some idea. And they won't provide a systematic presentation of everything the Bible says about any subject. Rather, they will create an opportunity for biblical truths to renew your heart and mind.

There are six studies in each guide. Our hope is that this will provide you with maximum flexibility in how you use these guides. Combining the guides in various ways will allow you to adapt them to your time schedule and to focus on the concerns most important to you or your group.

All of the studies in this series use a workbook format. Space is provided for writing responses to each question. This is ideal for personal study and allows group members to prepare in advance for the discussion. The guides also contain notes with suggestions on how to lead a group discussion. The notes provide additional background information on certain questions, give helpful tips on group dynamics and suggest ways to deal with problems that may arise during the discussion. These features equip someone with little or no experience to lead an effective discussion.

Suggestions for Individual Study

1. As you begin each study, pray that God would give you wisdom and courage through his Word.

2. After spending time in preparation, read and reread the passage to be studied.

3. Write your responses in the space provided or in a personal journal.

Writing can bring clarity and deeper understanding of yourself and God's Word. For the same reason, we suggest that you write out your prayers at various points in each study.

4. Most of the studies include questions that invite you to spend time in meditative prayer. The biblical text is communication addressed personally to us. Meditative prayer can enrich and deepen your experience of a biblical text.

5. After you have completed your study of the passage, you might want to read the leader's notes at the back of the guide to gain additional insight and information.

6. Share what you are learning with someone you trust. If you are not able to use these guides in a group you might want to consider participating in one of our online discussion groups at <www.lettinggodbegod.com>.

Suggestions for Group Study

Even if you have already done these studies individually, we strongly encourage you to find some way to do them with a group of other people as well. Although each person's journey is different, everyone's journey is empowered by the mutual support and encouragement that can only be found in a one-on-one or group setting. Several reminders may be helpful for participants in a group study.

1. Trust grows over time. If opening up in a group setting feels risky, realize that you do not have to share more than what feels safe to you. However, taking risks is a necessary part of growth. So do participate in the discussion as much as you are able.

2. Be sensitive to the other members of the group. Listen attentively when they talk. You will learn from their insights. If you can, link what you say to the comments of others so the group stays on the topic.

3. Be careful not to dominate the discussion. We are sometimes so eager to share what we have learned that we do not leave opportunity for others to respond. By all means participate! But allow others to do so as well.

4. Expect God to teach you through the passage being discussed and through the other members of the group. Pray that you will have a profitable time together.

5. We recommend that groups follow a few basic guidelines and that these guidelines be read at the beginning of each discussion session. The guidelines, which you may wish to adapt to your situation, are

☐ Anything said in the group is considered confidential and will not be discussed outside the group unless specific permission is given to do so.

☐ We will provide time for each person present to talk if he or she feels comfortable doing so.

☐ We will talk about ourselves and our own situations, avoiding conversation about other people.

☐ We will listen attentively to each other.

☐ We will be very cautious about giving advice.

☐ We will pray for each other.

If you are the discussion leader, you will find additional suggestions and helpful ideas for each study in the leader's notes. These are found at the back of the guide.

You might also want to consider participating in the online discussion forum for group leaders at <www.lettinggodbegod.com>.

1

The Promise of Hope

JEREMIAH 29:11-13

We need hope. We cannot go on without it. Without it our present, our past and our future are dark, frightening places. With it, there is light.

In this study we will explore God's promise of hope. The text is from a letter written by the prophet Jeremiah to "the surviving elders among the exiles and to the priests, the prophets and all the other people Nebuchadnezzar had carried into exile from Jerusalem to Babylon" (Jeremiah 29:1). It is a letter written to people who had every reason to lose hope. They had been defeated in war and carried away as captives to a distant land. This letter is a window to the way God responds to people whose situations could easily lead to hopelessness.

PREPARE

Think about times in your early years when you were promised something you wanted. What was it like to hope for that promise to come true?

What would it have been (or was it) like to have such promises forgotten and not kept?

What was it like to have such promises come true?

READ

11"For I know the plans I have for you," declares the LORD,
"plans to prosper you and not to harm you, plans to give you
hope and a future. 12Then you will call upon me and come
and pray to me, and I will listen to you. 13You will seek me and find me when
you seek me with all your heart." (Jeremiah 29:11-13)

STUDY

1. What title(s) would you give this text?

2. What does this text reveal about God?

3. What does this text reveal about the kind of relationship God wants to have with us?

---

4. List the individual promises made in this text.

---

5. Which of these promises do you especially need to hear?

---

6. What might make it difficult to trust these promises?

---

7. What might help you trust God's promise of a hope and a future?

---

8. Reread these verses, putting your name in the text several times. Hear God speak these words of promise directly to you.

9. What responses do you have to hearing this text in this way?

---

10. What specific gifts of hope do you especially need from God at this time?

Reflect

Spend some time of quiet reflecting on the images that come to mind when you think of your future. Write down whatever comes to mind—whether hopeful, frightening or neutral. As you look at these images, what feelings do they suggest you have about your future?

Respond

God promises us hope. We look toward a future blessed by God's loving, attentive presence with us. Each day this week spend a few minutes in quiet asking God to give you images of how God's love and blessing will be with you in the future. Keep a journal about whatever comes to mind during these times.

2

When All Hope Is Gone

MATTHEW 27:41-56

There are times when life seems utterly hopeless. In those times it seems that God has forgotten us. The only thing we can imagine in such times is despair. But in our moments of despair, when circumstances are overwhelming, God is present, loving us and working in powerful ways.

Perhaps the most profound time of darkness—when all reason to hope seemed to disappear—was when Jesus was crucified. The despair that Jesus' followers felt must have been terrible. Yet, in these terrible hours of darkness, God was doing a great work. In the text for this study we will explore these hours when it seemed like all hope was gone.

PREPARE

Think about a time when you felt hopeless. In your experience, what is the experience of hopelessness like—physically, mentally, emotionally, spiritually?

Think about a time when you felt hope-full. In your experience, what is the experience of hopefulness like—physically, mentally, emotionally, spiritually?

READ

41In the same way the chief priests, the teachers of the law and the elders mocked him. 42"He saved others," they said, "but he can't save himself! He's the King of Israel! Let him come down now from the cross, and we will believe in him. 43He trusts in God. Let God rescue him now if he wants him, for he said, 'I am the Son of God.'" 44In the same way the robbers who were crucified with him also heaped insults on him.

45From the sixth hour until the ninth hour darkness came over all the land. 46About the ninth hour Jesus cried out in a loud voice, "Eloi, Eloi, lama sabachthani?"*—which means, "My God, my God, why have you forsaken me?"*

47When some of those standing there heard this, they said, "He's calling Elijah."

48Immediately one of them ran and got a sponge. He filled it with wine vinegar, put it on a stick, and offered it to Jesus to drink. 49The rest said, "Now leave him alone. Let's see if Elijah comes to save him."

50And when Jesus had cried out again in a loud voice, he gave up his spirit.

51At that moment the curtain of the temple was torn in two from top to bottom. The earth shook and the rocks split. 52The tombs broke open and the bodies of many holy people who had died were raised to life. 53They came out of the tombs, and after Jesus' resurrection they went into the holy city and appeared to many people.

54When the centurion and those with him who were guarding Jesus saw the earthquake and all that had happened, they were terrified, and exclaimed, "Surely he was the Son of God!"

55Many women were there, watching from a distance. They had followed Jesus from Galilee to care for his needs. 56Among them were Mary Magdalene, Mary the mother of James and Joses, and the mother of Zebedee's sons. (Matthew 27:41-56)

STUDY

1. Read this text up to the point at which Jesus cried out in a loud voice and gave up his spirit. Read it as if you were there, standing with the large group of women who had come to care for Jesus. What did you experience as you read the text in this way?

2. How does the mocking of Jesus add to the hopelessness of this scene?

3. Jesus cried out, "My God, why have you forsaken me?" If you were there at the time, what reactions might you have had to this cry?

4. Think of a time when you felt forsaken by God or had fears that God might forsake you. What was that experience like?

5. How might fearing that we have been forsaken by God increase the experience of hopelessness?

6. How might it help you to remember that Jesus experienced a time of feeling forsaken by God?

---

7. Things are not always what they seem. Our moments of greatest despair are sometimes moments when God is at work in powerful ways. Think of a situation in which you were feeling hopeless but which turned out to be a time of positive change. What happened?

---

8. How might the events immediately after Jesus' death have affected his followers' experience of hopelessness?

---

9. How might it help you to know that God is at work, even in your times of despair?

10. In a time of quiet, ask God to remind you that he is at work to bring good in your life, even in areas that may seem hopeless to you right now. Write about your experience during this time of prayer.

Reflect

Spend some time reflecting on the times in your life when you have lost hope. Write about each experience and about how hope was restored.

Respond

Be aware each day this week of your experiences of hope and your experiences of hopelessness during the day. Ask God to open your heart and mind to receive gifts of hope. Keep a journal of your observations and experiences of praying in this way.

3

God's Response to Our Hopelessness

1 Kings 19:3-8

We are not always able to receive God's gift of hope. Sometimes we want to be left alone with our hopelessness. Sometimes we may even want to lay down and die. We may wonder in these times how God responds to us. How does the God of hope respond to our hopelessness?

This study examines God's specific, active, loving responses to one person's experience of hopelessness. This person was a man of great faith. His name was Elijah. God had done great miracles through Elijah. But in the text for this study, we will see that there was a time when Elijah lost all hope and wanted to die. As we will see, God did not shame Elijah or cheer him up or try to talk him out of his hopelessness. Instead, God responded to Elijah's hopelessness by caring for his needs.

Prepare

When you have experienced times of hopelessness, what responses did you receive from other people that were helpful to you?

When you have experienced times of hopelessness, what responses did you receive from others that were not helpful to you?

Read

[3]Elijah was afraid and ran for his life. When he came to
Beersheba in Judah, he left his servant there, [4]while he him-
self went a day's journey into the desert. He came to a broom
tree, sat down under it and prayed that he might die. "I have had enough,
Lord," he said. "Take my life; I am no better than my ancestors." [5]Then he lay
down under the tree and fell asleep.
All at once an angel touched him and said, "Get up and eat." [6]He looked
around, and there by his head was a cake of bread baked over hot coals, and
a jar of water. He ate and drank and then lay down again.
[7]The angel of the Lord came back a second time and touched him and
said, "Get up and eat, for the journey is too much for you." [8]So he got up and
ate and drank. Strengthened by that food, he traveled forty days and forty
nights until he reached Horeb, the mountain of God. (1 Kings 19:3-8)

Study

1. What title would you give this story?

2. How does Elijah express his hopelessness in his words?

3. How does Elijah express his hopelessness in his actions?

---

4. How do your experiences of hopelessness (or decreased hope) compare to Elijah's?

---

5. When you are feeling less than hopeful, what do you imagine that God is thinking and feeling toward you?

---

6. How do you imagine God might act toward you in those times?

---

7. How do your images of God's possible responses to you in times of hopelessness compare to God's response to Elijah in this text?

8. What significance do you see in the gifts that the angel brought to Elijah?

9. Put yourself in this story as Elijah. What might it be like to have an angel of the Lord care for you in these ways when you are feeling less than hopeful?

10. In a moment of quiet, tell God about your need for hope, and ask God to restore or strengthen your hope. Write whatever you sense God may be showing you.

Reflect

Spend some time reflecting on Psalm 34:18. Write a prayer in response to this verse.

Respond

Use the meditative prayer in question 10 every day this week. Keep a journal of what you sense God is showing you.

4

The God of Hope

Romans 15:1-7, 13

Hope is a wonderful gift. It fills us with energy. It keeps us engaged in life. It is like a candle burning steadily in a room that otherwise would have no light.

But as we know, there is much that seems to threaten our hope. Sometimes the candle flickers, sometimes it goes out. When we experience our hope fading and dying, we often feel that we are failing—failing to "keep the faith," failing to hang on. But hope is not an object we can hang on to. It is a gift that comes from God. God is our source of hope. We need to hang on to God. And when we cannot hang on, God hangs on to us—holding us in a loving heart.

God is the God of hope. To hang on to God is to hang on to hope. To be held by God is to be held by love. Love that has been with us in the past is with us today and will be with us in the future—love that redeems our lives, that brings good out of difficult circumstances; love that holds us and keeps us, no matter what.

Prepare

In your experience, what factors contribute to the experience of hopelessness?

In your experience, what factors contribute to the experience of hopefulness?

READ

[1]We who are strong ought to bear with the failings of the
weak and not to please ourselves. [2]Each of us should please
his neighbor for his good, to build him up. [3]For even Christ
did not please himself but, as it is written: "The insults of those who insult you
have fallen on me." [4]For everything that was written in the past was written to
teach us, so that through endurance and the encouragement of the Scriptures
we might have hope.

[5]May the God who gives endurance and encouragement give you a spirit of
unity among yourselves as you follow Christ Jesus, [6]so that with one heart and
mouth you may glorify the God and Father of our Lord Jesus Christ.

[7]Accept one another, then, just as Christ accepted you, in order to bring
praise to God. . . .

[13]May the God of hope fill you with all joy and peace as you trust in him, so
that you may overflow with hope by the power of the Holy Spirit. (Romans
15:1-7, 13)

STUDY

1. What two or three themes stand out to you in this text?

2. What thoughts do you have about the instructions for relating to each other that Paul gives in this text ?

3. Paul says the result of relating in this way is that we gain a sense of unity. How do you think these ways of relating might lead to unity?

---

4. Paul also suggests that these ways of relating create encouragement and hope. How do you see the dynamic between acting in ways that are loving and nonjudgmental and creating an environment of hope?

---

5. How does Paul describe God in this text?

---

6. How do these descriptions of God compare to how you think about God?

---

7. In a moment of quiet, be still before the God of encouragement and hope. Take in these gifts of encouragement and hope from God as you are able. Write about your experience in this time of reflection.

8. The last verse of this text is a prayer of blessing. It is a prayer that we would overflow with hope, joy and peace. What is the relationship between hope and joy and peace?

---

9. The last verse of this text also describes hope both as a gift from God and as a byproduct of our "trust in him" (our relying on God, our hope in God). How do you see the relationship between God's gift and our trust?

---

10. Use the last verse of this text as a prayer of blessing. Reread it with your name inserted in the text as often as possible. Spend a few minutes in quiet, asking God to grant you a vision of what your life would be like if you were overflowing with hope.

REFLECT

One of the names for God in Scripture is the God of Hope. Reflect again on what it means to you to have hope. Reflect on God as the source of this gift.

RESPOND

Use questions 7 and 10 every day this week as a focus for prayerful reflection. Keep a journal of what you sense God is showing you.

5

Receiving Hope from God

ROMANS 5:1-8

Our most fundamental reason for hopefulness is that we are loved. Our hope remains strong when we remember that no matter what happens, we are loved.

God is the God of hope because God is love. The text for this study reminds us that the hope that comes from God does not disappoint us because God loves us. Even when we see ourselves as God's enemies, God loves us. God reaches out to us. God gives his life for us. We are loved by God to a degree that is incomprehensible to us. It is a radical, unconditional, active, generous, abundant, unfailing love. God's love is sure. Absolutely sure. God's love is the basis of our hope.

PREPARE

Think of a time when you were hopeful about something and the hope was realized. How would you describe the experience of having your hope realized?

In what areas of your life have you experienced disappointment so often that you are now hesitant to allow yourself to hope?

READ

1Therefore, since we have been justified through faith, we
have peace with God through our Lord Jesus Christ, 2through
whom we have gained access by faith into this grace in
which we now stand. And we rejoice in the hope of the glory of God. 3Not only
so, but we also rejoice in our sufferings, because we know that suffering pro-
duces perseverance; 4perseverance, character; and character, hope. 5And hope
does not disappoint us, because God has poured out his love into our hearts by
the Holy Spirit, whom he has given us.

6You see, at just the right time, when we were still powerless, Christ died for
the ungodly. 7Very rarely will anyone die for a righteous man, though for a
good man someone might possibly dare to die. 8But God demonstrates his own
love for us in this: While we were still sinners, Christ died for us. (Romans 5:1-8)

STUDY

1. What title would you give this text?

2. What is Paul saying about the basis of our hope?

3. What experiences of God's love for you contribute to your hope in life?

4. This text tells us that hope can also come out of our sufferings. What does Paul say about the relationship between our sufferings and hope?

---

5. How have you seen this to be true in your life?

---

6. Paul also says that the hope we have in God does not (and will not) disappoint us. How would you summarize what Paul is saying about this (vv. 5-8)?

---

7. How would you describe the relationship between experiencing hopelessness and being afraid that God does not love you?

---

8. How would you describe the relationship between experiencing hope and knowing you are loved by God?

9. In a moment of quiet, reflect on verse 5 of this text. Ask God to pour love into you and fill you with the hope that comes from knowing you are absolutely and always loved. Write about your experience in this time of reflection.

---

10. What specific gifts of hope do you especially need from God at this time?

REFLECT

Read Romans 8:31-39. Nothing can "separate us from the love of God that is in Christ Jesus our Lord." Reflect on this truth as the basis of the hope God wants you to receive.

RESPOND

Use the meditative prayer in question 9 every day this week. Keep a journal of what you sense God is showing you.

6

Living in Hope

Psalm 146

We can live in hope because God is our hope.

The text for this study offers a beautiful and powerful reminder of the character of God. It reminds us that God is the Creator of all things in heaven and earth. It reminds us that God faithfully, compassionately cares for all of creation. It reminds us that God's love is active, all-inclusive and full of compassion—that God reaches out in love and power to the oppressed, the hungry, the prisoner and the blind, those who are discouraged, the fatherless and the widow.

We can live in hope because the reason for our hope is God. God made us, God loves us, and God—in the words of Psalm 146—"remains faithful forever." As we grow in trust that this is truly who God is, we will be able to more fully let God be the God of hope in our lives.

Prepare

As you have worked through these Bible studies, what experiences have you had of seeing God as a God of hope?

As you have worked through these studies, what experiences have you had of receiving hope from God?

READ

1 *Praise the LORD.*

Praise the LORD, O my soul.
2 *I will praise the LORD all my life;*
I will sing praise to my God as long as I live.

3 *Do not put your trust in princes,*
in mortal men, who cannot save.
4 *When their spirit departs, they return to the ground;*
on that very day their plans come to nothing.
5 *Blessed is he whose help is the God of Jacob,*
whose hope is in the LORD his God,
6 *the Maker of heaven and earth,*
the sea, and everything in them—
the LORD, who remains faithful forever.
7 *He upholds the cause of the oppressed*
and gives food to the hungry.
The LORD sets prisoners free,
8 *the LORD gives sight to the blind,*
the LORD lifts up those who are bowed down,
the LORD loves the righteous.
9 *The LORD watches over the alien*
and sustains the fatherless and the widow,
but he frustrates the ways of the wicked.

10 *The LORD reigns forever,*
your God, O Zion, for all generations.

Praise the LORD. (Psalm 146)

STUDY

1. What themes stand out to you in this text?

2. What contrast does the psalmist make between finding our source of hope in other people versus finding our source of hope in God?

3. Where are you tempted to look for hope, other than to God?

4. In your experience, what happens when you make people your source of hope?

5. According to the psalmist, God does many things that might encourage us to put our hope in God. What are these things?

6. What do these activities on God's part tell us about God?

---

7. In what ways does your personal experience of God match the description of God in this text?

In what ways is your personal experience of God different from this description of God?

---

8. Reread the text, inserting your name in the text as often as possible. Let these descriptions of God's powerful, loving, active presence in your life speak to you. Write about your experience of hearing the text in this way.

---

9. In a moment of quiet, reflect on the descriptions in this psalm of God's activities on our behalf. Ask God to grant you a vision of what it would be like to live daily in hope based on God's powerful, personal love for you. Write whatever comes to mind.

---

10. The psalm begins with words of praise to God. Spend some time writing words of praise for the ways in which God has given you gifts of hope.

REFLECT

Select one of the descriptions of God from this text. Spend some time reflecting on this truth about God. Write a prayer, a poem or a song, or create a piece of visual art that expresses this aspect of God's character.

RESPOND

Living in hope is possible when we remember God's loving acts on our behalf. Each day ask for the eyes to see and a heart to receive God's gifts of hope for you that day. Each night before you sleep, thank God for any way in which you experienced God's loving presence giving you gifts of hope during the day.

Leader's Notes

You may be experiencing a variety of feelings as you anticipate leading a group through this study guide. You may feel inadequate for the task and afraid of what will happen. If this is the case, know you are in good company. Many other small group leaders share this experience. It may help you to know that your willingness to lead is a gift to the other group members. It might also help if you tell them about your feelings and ask them to pray for you. Realize as well that the other group members share the responsibility for the group. And realize that it is the Spirit's work to bring insight, comfort, healing and recovery to group members. Your role is simply to provide guidance to the discussion. The suggestions listed below will help you to provide that guidance.

Preparing to Lead

1. Develop realistic expectations of yourself as a small group leader. Do not feel that you have to "have it all together." Rather, commit yourself to an ongoing discipline of honesty about your own needs. As you grow in honesty about your own needs, you will grow as well in your capacity for compassion, gentleness and patience with yourself and with others. As a leader you can encourage an atmosphere of honesty by being honest about yourself.

2. Pray. Pray for yourself. Pray for the group members. Invite the Spirit to be present as you prepare and as you meet.

3. Read the text several times.

4. Take your time to thoughtfully work through each question, writing out your answers.

5. After completing your personal study, read through the leader's notes for the study you are leading. These notes are designed to help you in several ways. First, they tell you the purpose the authors had in mind while writing the study. Take time to think through how the questions work together to accomplish that purpose. Second, the notes provide you with additional background information or comments on some of the questions. This information can be useful when people have difficulty understanding or answering a question. Third, the leader's notes can alert you to potential problems you may encounter during the study.

6. If you wish to remind yourself during the group discussion of anything mentioned in the leader's notes, make a note to yourself below that question in your study guide.

Leading the Study

1. Begin on time. You may want to open in prayer, or have a group member do so.

2. Be sure everyone has a study guide. Decide as a group whether you want people to do the study on their own ahead of time. If your time together is limited, it will be helpful for people to prepare in advance.

3. At the beginning of your first time together, explain that these studies are meant to be discussions, not lectures. Encourage the members of the group to participate. However, do not put pressure on those who may be hesitant to speak during the first few sessions. Clearly state that people do not need to share anything they do not feel safe sharing. Remind people that it will take time to trust each other.

4. Read aloud the group guidelines listed in the front of the guide. These commitments are important in creating a safe place for people to talk and trust and feel.

5. Read aloud the introductory paragraphs at the beginning of the discussion for the day. This will orient the group to the passage being studied.

6. If the group does not prepare in advance, approximately ten minutes will be needed for individuals to work on the "Prepare" section. This is designed to help group members focus on some aspect of their personal experience. Hopefully it will help group members to be more aware of the frame of reference and life experience that we bring to the text. This time of personal reflection can be done prior to the group meeting or as the first part of the meeting. The prepare questions are not designed to be for group discussion, but you might begin by asking the group what they learned from the prepare questions.

7. Read the passage aloud. You may choose to do this yourself, or someone else may read if he or she has been asked to do so prior to the study.

8. As you begin to ask the questions in the guide, keep several things in mind. First, the questions are designed to be used just as they are written. If you wish, you may simply read them aloud to the group. Or you may prefer to express them in your own words. However, unnecessary rewording of the questions is not recommended.

Second, the questions are intended to guide the group toward understanding and applying the main idea of the study. The authors of the guide have stated the purpose of each study in the leader's notes. You should try to understand how the study questions and the biblical text work together to lead the group in that direction.

There may be times when it is appropriate to deviate from the study guide. For example, a question may have already been answered. If so, move on to the next question. Or someone may raise an important question not covered in the guide. Take time to discuss it! The important thing is to use discretion. There may be many routes you can travel to reach the goal of the study. But the easiest route is usually the one the authors have suggested.

9. Don't be afraid of silence. People need time to think about the question before formulating their answers.

10. Don't be content with just one response. Ask, "What do the rest of you think?" or "Anything else?" until several people have given answers to the question.

11. Acknowledge all contributions. Try to be affirming whenever possible. Never reject an answer. If it seems clearly wrong to you, ask: "Which part of the text led you to that conclusion?" or "What do the rest of you think?"

12. Don't expect every answer to be addressed to you, even though this will probably happen at first. As group members become more at ease, they will begin to interact more effectively with each other. This is a sign of a healthy discussion.

13. Don't be afraid of controversy. It can be very stimulating. Differences can enrich our lives. If you don't resolve an issue completely, don't be frustrated. Move on and keep it in mind for later. A subsequent study may resolve the problem.

14. Stick to the passage under consideration. It should be the source for answering the questions. Discourage the group from unnecessary cross-referencing. Likewise, stick to the subject and avoid going off on tangents.

15. Periodically summarize what the group has said about the topic. This helps to draw together the various ideas mentioned and gives continuity to the study. But be careful not to use summary statements as an opportunity to give a sermon!

16. End each study with a prayer time. You will want to draw on the themes of your study and individual prayer and meditation as you now pray together. There are several ways to handle this time in a group. The person who leads each study could lead the group in a prayer, or you could allow time for group participation. Remember that some members of your group may feel uncomfortable about participating in public prayer. It might be helpful to discuss this with the group during your first meeting and to reach some agreement about how to proceed.

Listening to Emotional Pain

These Bible study guides are designed to take seriously the pain and struggle that is part of life. People will experience a variety of emotions during these studies. Part of your role as group leader will be to listen to emotional pain. Listening is a gift that you can give to a person who is hurting. For many people it is not an easy gift to give. The following suggestions will help you to listen more effectively to people in emotional pain.

1. Remember that you are not responsible to take the pain away. People in helping relationships often feel that they are being asked to make the other person feel better. This is usually related to the helper's own anxiety about painful feelings.

2. Not only are you not responsible to take the pain away, but one of the things people need most is an opportunity to face and to experience the pain in their life. They may have spent years denying their pain and running from it. Healing can come when we are able to face our pain in the presence of someone who cares about us. Rather than trying to take the pain away, then, commit yourself to listening attentively as it is expressed.

3. Realize that some group members may not feel comfortable with others' expressions of sadness or anger. You may want to acknowledge that such emotions are uncomfortable but that part of the growth process is to learn to feel and allow others to feel.

4. Be very cautious about giving answers and advice. Advice and answers may make you feel better or competent, but they may also minimize peoples' problems and their painful feelings. Simple solutions rarely work, and they can easily communicate "You should be better now" or "You shouldn't really be talking about this."

5. Be sure to communicate direct affirmation any time people talk about their painful emotions. It takes courage to talk about our pain because it creates anxiety for us. It is a great gift to be trusted by those who are struggling.

Study Notes

The following notes refer to the questions in the Bible study portion of each study.

Study 1. The Promise of Hope. Jeremiah 29:11-13.

Purpose: To hear God's promise to give us hope.

Question 1. The purpose of this question is to provide an overview of the text.

Welcome a variety of titles.

Question 2. This text reveals a God who is actively and intimately involved in our lives—a God who knows us personally, loves us and wants to give us good gifts.

Question 3. According to this text, the relationship God is seeking with us is one in which we talk to him and he listens to us, one in which God attends to us and offers us good gifts. It is an intimate relationship, one that is central to who we are.

Question 4. God promises to (1) prosper us, (2) not harm us, (3) give us hope, (4) give us a future, (5) listen to us, and (6) be found by us.

Question 5. Give participants time to reflect on these promises and imagine receiving these good gifts from God. Some people may need to hear all of these promises. Others may focus on only one or two of these promises.

Question 6. Many people have had promises made and broken by important people in their lives. They may even feel that they have had this same kind of experience with God. Trusting promises of this magnitude is not necessarily easy. This does not need to be a cause for shame or fear. God knows—better than we do—the reasons we may have difficulty trusting. Encourage participants to explore their fears and hesitations about trusting these promises.

Question 7. There are things that can build our faith. One faith builder is hearing other people's stories about God's work in their lives, or retelling our own stories of how God has been faithful in the past. Group participants may have other ideas about what is helpful to them. You might want to take some time to put some of these ideas into action.

Question 8. You may want to go around the group, giving each person a chance to read the text aloud in this way, or you may want to give individuals time to quietly read the text in this way, or you may want to break into groups of two and have participants read the text in this way for themselves or for each other.

Question 9. It can be a very powerful thing to hear a direct promise of hope from God. However, people will have a variety of responses. Some may feel doubtful. Some may feel numb. Others may be moved. Others may feel grateful or strengthened in their hope. Encourage honesty, welcoming a diversity of thoughts and feelings.

Study 2. When All Hope Is Gone. Matthew 27:41-56.

Purpose: To explore the experience of hopelessness.

Question 1. The purpose of this question is to help participants enter the story and empathize with those who were there. These women had probably been healed by Jesus in the past. Certainly they had been profoundly changed by his love. They had been following Jesus, placing all hope for the future in him. To stand at a distance and watch him die must have been a terrifying experience of helplessness and confusion. They must have felt deep shock and despair. It may have felt like the end of all hope.

Question 2. The mocking heightens the sense that evil is winning. It adds to the spiritual despair of this already terrible scene.

Question 3. This must have been both heartbreaking and frightening to the followers of Jesus who were there while he suffered. They had observed in the years that they had known Jesus that he clearly had an intimate, direct and powerful relationship with God. Was God forsaking him? Was God forsaking them? Was there any hope in this world?

Question 4. You may want to be prepared to share briefly and personally to open the way for other group members to feel safe sharing. Not everyone will relate to such an experience, but many will. If the group has not prepared ahead of time, you may want to give participants a few minutes to reflect and write about this question before beginning the discussion.

Question 5. The bottom line about experiencing hope in this world—especially as people of faith—is that we have some sense that God is in this with us. If we feel forsaken by God we will likely see ourselves as being punished or rejected; we will likely feel frightened and hopeless for the present and the future.

Question 6. Some people may think that Jesus' experience of being "forsaken" by God is so unique in its meaning that it cannot be profitably compared to our own subjective experiences of abandonment by God. While this way of emphasizing the uniqueness of Jesus may seem to honor Jesus, the text does *not* make this point. The biblical record makes it very clear that Jesus' experiences were like our own in every way except "without sin" (see Hebrews 4). Jesus knows what feeling forsaken by God feels like—because he experienced it himself. This can be a great comfort to us because Jesus can emphathize with us; it can help us when we feel guilty or ashamed for feeling this way and it can help us know we are not alone when we feel this way.

Question 7. This is an important time of sharing because remembering these stories of redemption can help us regain perspective and hope. Encourage members to write or reflect for a few minutes about a situation like this in their lives.

Question 8. A great deal seems to have happened immediately after Jesus died. (1) The curtain in the temple, which represented limitations on access to God, was torn in half, indicating that Jesus' death somehow was making possible direct access to God. (2) There was a significant earthquake. (3)

Holy people who were buried in tombs around the city were raised to life and visited people in the city, telling people about this man Jesus. (4) The men who were directly involved in Jesus' execution responded to the events that took place with a realization that they had killed the Son of God.

In this hour when God seemed to disappear, these are evidences that God was doing an unprecedented work. In this hour of despair, God was filling the word *hope* with deeper, richer meaning than we can comprehend.

Question 9. This possibility changes everything. It introduces hope into every situation. The more deeply we are able to trust this reality, the deeper our hope will be.

In an interview with Bill Moyers, Desmond Tutu, the Anglican archbishop of South Africa, talked about the days of greatest despair during apartheid. In the worst of times, he was able to hold onto a vision that allowed him to say to apartheid's leaders, "It is not too late to join the winning side." This is the kind of hope that becomes possible in our lives when we know that God is at work—even in times which seem hopeless.

Question 10. Give group members a few minutes alone to pray and reflect. Encourage participants to share personally and specifically (if they feel comfortable) about their experience in this time of prayer.

Study 3. God's Response to Our Hopelessness. 1 Kings 19:3-8.

Purpose: To see God's loving response to our hopelessness.

Question 2. Elijah expresses his hopelessness in words by asking to die. He tells God that he has had enough. He is tired of life, tired of the struggle. He thinks of himself as no better than his ancestors. He feels that God should kill him.

Question 3. Elijah expresses his hopelessness in actions by isolating himself—going out in the desert alone. And he expresses it by lying down and going to sleep. Both isolation and escape through sleep are common expressions of hopelessness.

Question 4. Encourage participants to spend a few minutes reflecting on their experiences of hopelessness or decreased hope so that they can compare and contrast their experiences with Elijah's experience.

Question 5. It is a fairly common experience for people to imagine that God reacts with impatience and even anger when we are feeling hopeless. Some people may think God expects us to be grateful, to maintain a balanced perspective, to never complain or get discouraged. Allow group members to brainstorm a variety of responses, which they imagine God might have toward them in times when they feel hopeless. Some may expect God to respond with compassion and support, as God does in this text. Some may expect God to respond with anger. Invite a full range of responses.

Question 6. People who expect God to be impatient or angry when they are losing hope may expect God to act by lecturing, scolding, withdrawing, abandoning, withholding or punishing. Those with a more positive perspective of God may imagine that God will be compassionate and loving. Many may find they have conflicting views of God—both loving and rejecting.

Question 7. God's response to Elijah's hopelessness is nurturing and patient. God sends angels. God feeds Elijah. God gives Elijah water. God lets him sleep twice and then gently nudges him to move out of this place of isolation and despair.

Question 8. The angel brought simple, practical gifts that would restore Elijah's physical strength and that communicated in tangible ways that he was loved and valued by God.

Question 9. Encourage group members to put themselves in the story and to see themselves being given these good gifts—or other good gifts from God. Allow a full range of responses to this experience.

Question 10. Allow enough time for people to pray and reflect individually. Then invite group participants to share what they experienced.

Study 4. The God of Hope. Romans 15:1-7, 13.

Purpose: To know God as the God of hope.

Question 1. The purpose of this question is to help participants get an overview of the text and to sort out some of the major points that are being made here. The major themes have to do with unity and God's gifts of encouragement and hope.

Question 2. Paul says to bear with the failings of other people, to act in ways that please and help the other person. That might sound passive or codependent, but it is important to understand that the context suggests Paul's intention is to discourage attacking and judging others.

Paul is giving advice about living in community, about practicing grace in our relationships. This letter was written to both Jews and Gentiles. The Jews tended to see themselves as God's chosen ones and to see the Gentiles as untouchables. Now they are living in community with Gentiles as Christians. They come from very different cultures. They are prejudiced toward each other. There is much room for conflict. Paul is reminding them what love looks like in this context.

Question 3. Paul is reminding the Jews and the Greeks that they have lived as enemies in the past. They have not respected or valued each other. They have acted in ways that fostered a sense of separation. Now they need to act in ways that close the gap so there is no sense of separation—being respectful, understanding, accepting and encouraging toward each other.

Question 4. Being judged, hated, misunderstood, looked down on spiritually—or in any other way—creates discouragement and hopelessness. Being embraced, respected, heard and valued is what creates encouragement and hope.

Question 5. God is described in this text as the God who gives endurance and encouragement, as the one who accepts us, and as the God of hope.

Question 6. Allow participants an opportunity to reflect on these truths about God. How do these truths challenge or stretch their views of God?

Question 7. Give participants time to pray and reflect individually and then to share with the group what they sensed as they prayed.

Question 8. Encourage a variety of reflections on the interrelationship of these wonderful gifts—hope, joy and peace. Explore the ways in which encouraging one of these gifts increases the others as well.

Question 9. The relationship between God's gift of hope and our trust in God is the relationship between being given a gift and receiving that gift. Receiving is an act of trust. The more we actively receive, or trust, the deeper that receiving becomes.

Study 5. Receiving Hope from God. Romans 5:1-8.

Purpose: To receive hope from God.

Question 1. The purpose of this question is to gain an overview of the text. Invite a variety of ideas.

Question 2. Paul is saying that God is the source of our hope. God's glory—all that God is—is the reason for our hope. He is saying we can be joyful because our hope is based in God's love and goodness. We can celebrate this hope.

Question 3. Invite group members to share how they have experienced God's love and goodness and how this has given them a reason to hope. Not all members will relate to this. Make opportunity for the full range of experiences to be expressed without judgment.

Question 4. Paul is saying that when we experience difficulties we discover and develop strengths in ourselves—or gifts of strength from God—which allow us to persevere and develop character in us. The character that develops produces hope. Invite a discussion about how this might happen. One way of looking at this is that when we learn to persevere—to hang in there—during hard times, we learn to not give up. Hope is a kind of not giving up. It is as if we actually practice hope—we make *hope* a verb rather than a noun in times of suffering.

Question 5. Invite people to share times when they have put this kind of "not giving up" into practice and discovered a deeper reservoir of hope and strength in their hearts and minds.

Question 6. This is a very moving and powerful text. The hope we have in God does not disappoint us, Paul says, "because God has poured his love into our hearts by the Holy Spirit." He goes on to say that God loves us no matter what. Even when we see ourselves as God's enemies, God loves us.

Question 7. The connection between hope and knowing that God's love is certain is difficult for many of us. The reason for this is that to some degree most of us struggle with trusting the full reality of God's love. Sometimes trusting that God loves us is more difficult than other times. There is often a direct correlation between being afraid we are not loved and feeling hopeless. As much as possible, make it safe for people to discuss how they have experienced this in some way in their life.

Question 8. It is important to reflect on the opposite side of the coin. Trusting that we are loved by God—personally and unshakably—provides deep hope. It does not remove life's problems. It does not mean we are free from pain. But we are better able to hang on to hope in the midst of it all. Again, invite group members to share as personally as they are able about their experience of this relationship between hope and love.

Question 9. Give people time to pray, reflect and write individually. Invite them to share their experience with the group or in subgroups of two or three. Some people may find this time of prayer meaningful, some may find it discouraging. Make it safe for people to struggle with whatever might come up for them by listening well and by thanking them for their openness.

Study 6. Living in Hope. Psalm 146.

Purpose: To explore the possibility of living in hope.

Question 1. The themes have to do with trusting in God and with who God is—with why God is truly trustworthy. Individuals may have unique ways of describing this theme.

Question 2. The contrast between making people the basis of our hope versus making God the reason for our hope is quite dramatic. People do not have the power to save or protect us. People are limited. God has infinite power and love.

Question 3. It is not only other people that we mistakenly look to as the basis of hope. We may find ourselves putting our trust in our bank accounts, or our talents, or our hard work. Encourage people to share freely where they might be tempted to mistakenly place their hope.

Question 5. The psalmist gives us powerful reminders of the importance of putting our hope in the Lord our God. God is the Creator of all things in heaven and earth; God cares about and takes care of the oppressed and the hungry; God frees the prisoner; God heals the blind; God lifts up those who are "bowed down"—discouraged or despairing or ashamed. God loves the righteous (those who live in relationship with God). God takes care of the alien, the fatherless and the widow. God frustrates the ways of the wicked.

Question 6. This is a reminder of God's power and of God's love. It is a powerful and intimate portrait of God's attentiveness and active care for each of us personally. It tells us that God loves us, that God provides for us, that God sees our needs and responds to us, and that God is merciful and kind.

Question 7. Some people may find themselves surprised or moved by this powerful portrait of God's compassionate, caring, powerful love. Invite an honest sharing about how this revelation of God matches—or doesn't match—people's personal experience of God.

Question 8. The purpose of this question is to help people make this text more personal, to put themselves in this list of those God cares for and responds to. You may want to divide into pairs and have people read the text to each other or aloud to themselves. Encourage people to give themselves a few minutes to absorb the impact of this text in this personal way.

Question 9. Give people time to pray and reflect and write individually. Invite them to share their experience with the group or in subgroups of two or three.

Question 10. You may want to use this as a time of celebration and closure of this time of study together.

Online Resources

If you would like to share your experience using this Bible study with other people, we invite you to join us online at

<www.lettinggodbegod.com>

At the website you will be able to sign up to receive a free daily meditation written by Dale and Juanita Ryan.

Additional resources of interest to some users of these studies can be found at the online home of the Ryans:

<www.christianrecovery.com>